FATHER FIGURE

JON SIMPSON

TABLE OF CONTENTS

DEDICATION

Mom,

You've always guided me in the spirit of the Lord and shown up for me in every moment. I'll spend my life honoring the grace you've taught me.

I thank God for you every single day.

Kayle,

You are the queen of my heart. God knew I needed a strong, beautiful woman to sharpen me and keep me growing. You amaze me every day. I'm so blessed to have you in my life, and I couldn't have done this without you.

Dad (Jon),

It's been a long road to get here. I'm proud of your sobriety, and I pray God continues to strengthen you in your fight. I hope this book helps you understand my perspective, and more than anything, I hope it makes you proud. I love you.

Dad (Chris),

I know we haven't spoken in years. But if this book has found its way into your hands, I believe that's not by accident.

Only God could make that happen.

There's a reason you're holding it. I love you, and I understand more than you may think.

My Children,

You are my inspiration to keep going and to figure this fatherhood journey out. I love you more than words can express. I promise I'm giving this my very best. I hope one day this book brings you clarity, perspective, and maybe even a smile. You are my greatest adventure.

See you at dinner.

PREFACE: LIFE'S AN ADVENTURE, WHETHER YOU HAVE TIME FOR IT OR NOT

Life is busy. Fatherhood, even more so.

For those of us trying to balance demanding work schedules with a genuine desire to be present, stable, and involved at home, it can feel overwhelming. You want to provide. You want to lead. You want to be there. And sometimes it feels like all three are pulling you in different directions.

This book isn't a miracle "how-to" manual with all the answers, because I'm not qualified to write that, and I'm not sure anyone is. Fatherhood isn't something you master; it's something you grow into. What this book *is* meant to be is a companion on that journey. Something you can come back to when you need a reset, a reminder, or a different perspective.

Short enough to be practical. Thoughtful enough to offer real value.

Because the truth is, this world needs great fathers.

Your children need one.

Your wife needs you to be one.

And whether you realize it or not, the effort you put into becoming that man impacts everything around you.

Most of what you'll find in this book won't just lead to happier kids, it will lead to a stronger, healthier relationship with your wife too. There's something powerful about a man who shows up intentionally for his family. A man who isn't just physically present, but emotionally engaged. It builds trust. It builds connection. It builds a home that people actually *want* to be in.

On the flip side, when fatherhood is neglected, it doesn't stay contained, it spills over. It shows up in tension, in distance, and often in the breakdown of relationships.

Because the reality is, your wife needs a version of what your children need too: attention, presence, and emotional connection.

If you're reading this and thinking it might be too late, that you've missed too many moments or made too many mistakes, I want to be clear: It's not too late.

Even if you're reading this for the first time as an empty nester, there is still time to show up differently. The fact that you're here, reading this, means something. It means you care. And that alone puts you ahead of where you think you are.

That said, there's one important thing to keep in mind.

Don't read this and then walk out into the living room announcing that everything's going to change starting today. Don't make big promises about the man you're about to become.

If it's real, you won't need to say it.

Show them.

Let your actions speak. Let your consistency build the story. There's something far more powerful about your family *noticing* the change than being told about it.

It removes the pressure, makes it more natural, and most importantly, it makes it genuine.

You don't need a speech.

You don't need a declaration. You just need to start.

The beautiful part is, you can do that right now, without promising a thing.

And while I'm not here to hand out empty praise, I will say this:

Starting matters.

Choosing to reflect, to learn, and to be intentional about the kind of father you are, that's a step a lot of men never take. If you follow through, it can change everything.

I wish someone had handed something like this to my dads. Their lives, and our relationships, might look very different today.

But that's the point.

We don't get to rewrite where we came from. We *do* get to decide where we're going.

Let's get to work!

CHAPTER 1: WHERE THIS COMES FROM

Before you take advice from anyone about being a father, it's worth understanding where that advice is coming from. Fatherhood isn't something you study from a distance, it's something you experience, absorb, and often spend years trying to make sense of. The way a man shows up as a father is almost always shaped by the fathers who came before him.

My story is complicated, but not uncommon.

I was born to two teenagers. My mom was sixteen, my dad eighteen, both still in high school, both still figuring out who they were, let alone how to raise a child. My father was, in many ways, a typical young guy. He loved sports, but over time that passion gave way to something else, partying, drinking, and chasing the energy of being the life of the room. By his early twenties, that lifestyle had hardened into a serious drinking problem.

Not long after my younger sister was born, my mom reached her limit. Promises of change had come and gone too many times. When I was four years old, she packed us up and moved into my grandfather Rick's house, stepping into the unknown as a single mother of two.

Eventually, she met my stepfather, Chris. But before that chapter really began, my childhood was already split in two, life at my mom's during the week, and every other weekend at my dad's.

At my father's, much of our time revolved around the family business, a feed store and lawn-and-garden operation run with my grandfather Kurt. It sat on forty acres of land where they grew pumpkins and corn. Those moments, working, observing, being around my grandparents, left a mark on me in a good way. I learned about hard work, problem-solving, and responsibility. Those were real lessons, and they mattered.

But outside of that environment, things looked very different.

Home life with my dad was unstable. There were nights in a run-down apartment, issues with mice, and a revolving door of relationships that often ended in arguments or worse. Alcohol was always present. Dinner was whatever was quick and easy, kids' meals or frozen dinners, while the night usually ended the same way: with him passed out.

He remarried at one point, blending families in a way that never really worked. That marriage ended quickly, leaving behind more distance, more confusion, and half-siblings I haven't seen since they were toddlers. Somewhere in those years came multiple drunk driving charges, a permanently suspended license, and decisions that only deepened the chaos.

This isn't shared to place blame; it's simply the reality of what I saw growing up. My father has been sober for a couple of years now, and as an adult, I'm still trying to rebuild trust and figure out what a relationship with him looks like today.

While that was one side of my upbringing, the other came through my stepfather.

Chris entered our lives when my mom was just twenty-one, raising two young kids on her own. In many ways, he was exactly what she needed at that time. He was a journeyman plumber with a strong work ethic and a clear goal of building something for himself. I spent time working alongside him during summers and weekends, learning firsthand what it meant to earn money and take pride in your work.

He showed up in ways my biological father didn't; steady, reliable, and committed to providing. For a while, things felt like they were falling into place. My mom and Chris bought a home, and our family grew as more kids were added. There was a sense of excitement, of building something together. But over time, the tone shifted.

What started as energy and ambition slowly turned into exhaustion and tension. Long workweeks led to weekends where he needed space, quiet, and distance. The house became something you had to tiptoe around. Conversations were short, emotions were controlled, and anything deeper than surface level was often left unspoken.

He wasn't a man who expressed how he felt. Everything was practical, matter-of-fact, this is how things are, this is how they're going to be. And while that approach may have been meant to create stability, it created distance instead.

Eventually, that emotional disconnect took its toll. The marriage fell apart, his career unraveled, and our relationship followed. When I stood up for my mom during their divorce, it became a line that couldn't be crossed back. To this day, we don't speak.

These are condensed versions of much longer, more complicated stories. And while they've shaped me, this book isn't about dwelling on what was missing. It's about what can be built moving forward.

Because here's the truth: you don't need a perfect example of fatherhood to become a great father. Sometimes, the most powerful lessons come from seeing what not to do.

I had one father who showed me what happens when responsibility is avoided, and another who showed me what happens when emotion is withheld. Between the two, I was given a blueprint, not of what to follow, but of what to improve upon.

And that's what this book is about.

It's about choosing to lead differently. It's about learning to provide not just physically, but emotionally.

It's about becoming the kind of father your children don't have to recover from.

Because at the end of the day, fatherhood isn't about perfection, it's about intention. And the choice to show up better than what you were shown is where it all begins.

CHAPTER 2: MY OWN JOURNEY INTO FATHERHOOD

As I write this, I'm the proud father of three little girls, ten, five, and almost two. They are my whole world. Everything I've come to understand about fatherhood, growth, and purpose has been shaped by them. They are the reason I started asking deeper questions about the kind of man I want to be and the kind of father I need to become.

I share this life with my wife, Kayle, the other great love of my life. Together, we've built a family that continues to challenge me, refine me, and push me to be better every single day.

My journey into fatherhood didn't start the way I expected. My oldest daughter came into my life when she was three years old, from a previous relationship Kayle had. Before meeting her, I wasn't sure I even wanted kids. If I'm being honest, I leaned more toward not wanting them at all. My own experiences growing up left me uncertain about what kind of father I could be, or if I'd just repeat the same patterns I had witnessed.

But that changed the moment I got to know her.

Spending time with her flipped a switch in me. What started as curiosity turned into something much deeper. I found myself wanting more, not just more time with her, but more of a family, more responsibility, more purpose. She didn't just become my daughter; she became the reason I believed I could do this differently. She's the one who made me want to become the father I never had.

At the time, Kayle and I were building our life together from the ground up. I was working as a foreman for a local hardscape company, building patios and retaining walls. The hours were long, but the pay was steady enough that we could start thinking about our future in a real way.

Then life moved quickly, like it often does.

Kayle became pregnant with our daughter Ella, and not long after, we got engaged. By the time we were finally able to have the wedding we had envisioned, Ella was already two years old, running around, growing fast, and teaching me lessons about patience and presence I didn't even know I needed.

Around that same time, another major opportunity came my way: the chance to purchase the company I had spent seven years helping build. It was a big decision, equal parts exciting and terrifying. But it also felt like the right move. It gave us the stability to take the next steps, including buying a home in the country and continuing to grow our family.

In 2024, our daughter Madilynn was born.

Her arrival came at a time when I was still finding my footing as a business owner, learning how to lead a company while also trying to show up at home as the kind of husband and father my family deserved. It wasn't easy, but it forced me to grow in ways I never would have otherwise.

One of the biggest blessings in this season of life has been the flexibility my role now allows. Compared to when Ella was born, I'm able to be far more present, physically and emotionally. I can show up more, help more, and actually be part of the day-to-day moments that matter.

But I won't pretend this journey has been smooth.

Owning a business comes with pressure, financial, mental, and emotional. There are constant demands pulling at your time and attention. At the same time, fatherhood doesn't pause. Your kids need you. Your wife needs you. And if you're not careful, it can all start to feel overwhelming, even when your intentions are good.

We've also faced real challenges as a family. Post-partum depression is real, and it affects more than just one person, it impacts the entire household. Navigating that while trying to balance work, fatherhood, and being a supportive partner tested me in ways I wasn't prepared for.

The truth is, I'm not a master of any of this.

I'm still learning. Still adjusting. Still figuring it out as I go.

But what I have done is commit to paying attention, to listening to my wife, to checking in with myself, and to being honest about where I need to improve. Over time, I've started to develop some ideas, habits, and strategies that have helped me become a better partner, a better leader, and most importantly, a better father. That's what this book is about.

It's about sharing what I've learned so far, not as someone who has it all figured out, but as someone who's willing to do the work. If I can offer you a few insights, a few shortcuts, or even just a different perspective that helps you show up better for your family, then it's worth it.

Because this job, being a father, is the most rewarding one you'll ever have.

There's nothing in this world like your kids loving you and your wife genuinely wanting to be around you. That kind of connection doesn't happen by accident. It's built, day by day, through effort, awareness, and intention.

I'm writing this for you, but I'm also writing it for myself.

I'm a work in progress. And I plan to stay that way.

CHAPTER 3: THE STRENGTH TO BE SEEN: A FATHER'S RESPONSIBILITY BEYOND PROVISION

There are countless incredible things about becoming a father. It's a role filled with purpose, pride, and a deep sense of responsibility. Alongside that pride, though, comes a weight many men quietly carry, being the provider, the protector, the steady leader who guides his family through life's challenges. These expectations are often spoken about and widely accepted as the foundation of fatherhood.

But there's another responsibility, just as important, that often gets overlooked: the responsibility to be emotionally present, vulnerable, and expressive in a healthy, constructive way.

For many men, this doesn't come naturally. I know it hasn't for me. I grew up watching a version of masculinity built on being "tough", a man who didn't show emotion, didn't ask for help, and carried everything internally. Over time, that image began to crack. What once looked like strength started to resemble something else entirely: a quiet struggle, a life lived in silent desperation, too proud to admit when help was needed.

That experience isn't unique. Many of us were raised by "tough as nails" fathers who, despite their best intentions, modeled emotional suppression rather than emotional strength. The result? Strained relationships, disconnection, and a generation of men who were never taught how to process or express what they feel. It's time to change that.

As fathers, we are leaders in our households, not just in how we provide, but in how we live. Our children are always watching. They learn not only from what we say, but from how we react, how we handle stress, and how we express ourselves in difficult moments.

This isn't about abandoning stoicism or becoming overly reactive. There's still value in composure and restraint. But there's a difference between control and suppression. Bottling everything up, storing it away in the "deal with it later" box, doesn't make us stronger. It delays the inevitable, often until it comes out in unhealthy ways: anger, frustration, or emotional shutdown.

Instead, we should be showing our children a better way. We should demonstrate how to receive life's challenges, process them with intention, and respond in a way that reflects our values.

Because if a son grows up watching his father never express emotions, except through explosive anger, he learns that's what it means to be a man. And if a daughter grows up seeing that same behavior, she may come to accept it as normal in future relationships.

That cycle has consequences.

I've lived some of them myself, failed relationships, defensiveness, and a tendency to react rather than respond when I felt overwhelmed. But growth comes from awareness. I'm learning to approach emotions differently: to pause, to process, and to communicate calmly and honestly once I've found clarity. And the impact has been real, less resentment, more understanding, and stronger connections.

One of the biggest lies we tell ourselves is that things will slow down eventually, that once work settles or life gets easier, we'll have time to focus on what really matters. But life doesn't work that way. It's always busy. It's always messy. There's always something.

Being present, emotionally present, isn't something we can put off. It's part of the job.

Strength still matters. Life can be brutal at times, and resilience is essential. But real strength isn't just about enduring hardship, it's about being prepared for it. And one of the best ways to stay prepared is by understanding and expressing what we feel, rather than burying it.

Some storms pass quickly. Others linger. We don't always get to choose. But what we can choose is how we show up during them.

The greatest thing we can do for our families isn't to pretend we're unaffected, it's to show them that even when things are hard, we're steady, self-aware, and committed to working through it. It's about being emotionally available, not just physically present.

The era of "tough it out, don't talk about it" is coming to an end, and that's a good thing.

When you start living this way, something interesting happens. The tension lessens. The misunderstandings decrease. The people around you, your wife, your kids, begin to understand you better, and you understand them. You realize they were never trying to push your buttons; they just didn't know what you were carrying.

Communication builds connection.

Connection builds stronger families.

Being a father is one of the greatest adventures life offers. It's more than providing, it's about shaping the kind of humans your children will become. And that requires more than toughness. It requires honesty, vulnerability, and emotional leadership.

We don't just need strong men. We need strong, self-aware men who can raise good humans.

CHAPTER 4: MAKE ONE DAY...TODAY

Life is short. But the window of time when your kids *want* you, when they light up just because you walked into the room, is even shorter.

I grew up hearing a lot about "one day." *One day we'll go on that fishing trip.*

One day I'll take you elk hunting. One day, when we have the money, we'll really live.

You can probably guess how that story ends.

One day never came.

And the truth is, it never will, because eventually, life fills up. Responsibilities stack. Time moves on. And before you know it, you're no longer the kid waiting for "one day" … you're the father saying it.

That realization hit me hard.

Because now I have kids of my own. A full life. Real responsibilities. And I caught myself standing in the exact same place, pushing moments off, thinking I'd circle back when things slowed down.

But here's the reality: they don't slow down.

Work will always be there. Always. There is an unlimited supply of tasks, problems, and obligations waiting to take your time. Whether it's later that night, Monday morning, or next week, work will be ready for you. Your kids won't.

There's a limited number of times your five-year-old will ask you to jump on the trampoline. A limited number of nights they'll want to sit by a campfire and tell you stories they just made up on the spot. A limited number of chances to be their favorite person in the world.

And every time you say, "later," you're gambling with something you don't get back.

I've been guilty of it. Saying I'm busy. Saying I'm tired. Saying the bills don't pay themselves. Dressing up excuses in logic that sounds responsible, but feels hollow the second I see the look on my kid's face.

That quiet, deflated: "Okay, Dad."

And maybe worse, the look from your wife. The one that says everything without saying a word.

Here's the truth we don't always want to admit:

Being tired isn't a valid excuse.

Work isn't a valid excuse. Being out of shape, stressed out, or overwhelmed, none of it justifies missing the moments that matter most.

That doesn't mean you can't focus on work or take time for yourself. You absolutely should. But your family will be a whole lot more supportive of your individual needs when you're consistently showing up for theirs.

You're not just the provider.

You're the leader.

You're the tone-setter.

And whether you realize it or not, you're also the *captain of fun.*

Another place this really shows up is in the every-day, mundane parts of life, the errands, the obligations, the things you "have to do." If your wife asks for family time, the worst thing you can do is make it miserable by complaining your way through it.

You don't have to turn everything into Disney-land, but you can bring a better attitude. Make it light. Make it engaging. Be present. Even small things, like turning errands into a game or just being helpful without resistance, go a long way.

Because at the end of the day, your family doesn't just remember what you did. They remember how it felt to be around you while you were do-ing it.

One of the best things I've learned is simple: bring them into your world.

If I need to get something done, I'll make one of my kids my "helper." Does it slow things down? Of course. But it turns a task into time together. It creates opportunities to teach, to laugh, to connect, all while still moving forward.

And that list of things to do? It's never going away. Ever.

I'm writing this chapter at 3 a.m. because yesterday was packed, grocery shopping, ice skating, dinner, bath time, snacks, time with my wife. It was a full day.

But here's the part that matters: I showed up for it.

I was present. I was helpful. I wasn't dragging my feet or counting down the minutes. And because of that, I ended the night with something way better than crossed-off tasks, a connected family, a happy home, and a wife who actually *wanted* to spend time with me.

That beats the alternative every single time.

Because the alternative?

Is being the guy who's always miserable, always busy, always somewhere else mentally, and eventually, alone in it.

Look, I get it. Work is real. Pressure is real. Responsibility is real.

But if you can find time to watch basketball every night in March, or football three days a week for months… then you have time.

It's not about having time.

It's about how you choose to spend it.

So, stop waiting for "one day."
Make one day… today.

CHAPTER 5: SERVING YOUR FAMILY WITH A HAPPY HEART

As men, especially those of us who take the role of provider seriously, it's easy to feel like our efforts go unnoticed. By our wives. By our kids. It can feel like they don't understand what it takes just to maintain, let alone move forward.

While that feeling is real, it's often a misrepresentation of what's actually happening.

The truth is, our wives and our children *want* to love us. They *want* to appreciate what we do. But sometimes, we don't make it easy for them to show it.

Growing up, I saw this play out in my own home.

My stepfather worked hard to give us the best version of the American dream he could provide. Inside our modest home, he was a superhero. He showed up, he provided, and we looked up to him.

But over time, something shifted.

The stress of maintaining that life started to wear on him. The pressure became heavier. What was once driven by inspiration slowly became routine, and then eventually, a burden.

The cheerful, engaged man we admired became more distant. More irritable. More isolated.

Not because he didn't love us, but because he didn't know how to carry the weight in a healthy way.

The things he once did out of love started to come with expectation. Family time, help around the house, simple moments, those weren't just given anymore. They came with an unspoken need for recognition.

And when that recognition didn't come in the way he hoped, beyond a simple "Thanks, Dad" , frustration crept in.

Requests for help were met with resistance.

Conversations turned into lectures. Words like *"spoiled"* and *"you have no idea what it takes"* became common.

But here's what I've come to understand:

It was never that we didn't appreciate him.

We did.

We felt it deeply.

We just didn't always know how to express it in the way he needed, and over time, his stress convinced him that the appreciation wasn't there at all.

The real problem wasn't a lack of appreciation.

It was the weight he carried, and how it changed his heart.

What started as love-driven service slowly turned into resentment. Giving stopped feeling like a gift, and started feeling like an obligation that wasn't being properly recognized.

And that shift changes everything.

Your wife and your kids want to love you. They want to appreciate you.

They didn't change.

We did.

The good news?

It's not too late to fix it.

You don't need a grand gesture. You don't need a speech. You don't need them to suddenly "get it."

You simply go back.

Back to serving with a full heart.

Back to giving without expectation. Back to leading with love instead of keeping score.

It won't always feel easy, but it will work faster than you think.

At first, your family might not know what to do with the change. They may be cautious. Even a little unsure if it's real.

But once they begin to trust that it's consistent, that it's not temporary, you'll see something powerful happen.

The love you've been wanting… starts showing up.

Because it was never gone.

It was just waiting for a safe place to land.

Love produces love.

In fatherhood, love will always win.

In marriage, love will always win.

CHAPTER 6: MY JOURNEY TO BECOMING A FATHER FIGURE IN FAITH

Christianity was always present in the background of my life.

When I was young, my mom took us to Sunday school and ran our home in the spirit of the Lord. It was there, but it wasn't something I fully owned.

As I got older, that began to change.

Like a lot of teenagers, I carried anger, confusion, and questions I didn't know how to answer, especially when it came to my father. Trying to understand why my biological dad chose alcohol over his responsibilities became something that weighed on me more than I realized.

Without even realizing it, I made it my mission to understand him by becoming him.

In high school, I kept my grades up because it came easy. But once I had freedom, things shifted quickly. Smoking weed, drinking, chasing the next good time, what started as occasional became routine.

Then came college.

With no real accountability, everything escalated. What used to be weekend partying became weeknight chaos, with no intention of making it to class the next morning.

I became addicted to alcohol, but even more than that, I became addicted to being needed. The life of the party. The guy everyone wanted around.

I had become the exact version of my father I once questioned.

And I finally understood how easy it is to fall into that trap.

"There is a way that seems right to a man, but its end is the way to death.", Proverbs 14:12

But that version of "glory" doesn't last.

My grades dropped. My priorities disappeared. And when things started falling apart, so did the people around me. The same crowd that needed me when things were fun disappeared when I needed help.

I got kicked out of school.

Lost my apartment.

Couldn't hold a job.

And my solution?

I offered my weed dealer full-time help in exchange for a place to sleep.

That was rock bottom.

"For what does it profit a man to gain the whole world and forfeit his soul?", Mark 8:36

Eventually, I hit a point where I knew enough was enough.

I called home.

At 21 years old, I was back in my parents' basement, working at a gas station, a college dropout staring at the reality of where that path had led me.

This was the result of trying to walk life without God.

I wish I could say that's when everything changed.

It didn't.

I stayed stuck for a while.

A toxic relationship.

Another attempt at escape, this time working on Mackinac Island.

It looked like a fresh start, but it turned into more of the same, money, partying, distraction.

After two years, I chased another relationship and landed in Traverse City, Michigan.

Traverse City felt different.

For the first time in a long time, I started thinking seriously about who I wanted to be, and where I was headed.

I still wasn't fully walking with God, but I wasn't running from Him anymore either.

Looking back now, I can see it clearly.

"The Lord is patient… not wanting anyone to perish, but everyone to come to repentance.", 2 Peter 3:9

He was giving me time.

And then He changed everything.

He brought my wife into my life.

Kayle.

She wasn't perfect, but she was real. Strong. Resilient. Someone who had been through her own struggles but hadn't let them define her.

To me, she was everything.

And with her came her daughter.

Falling in love with that little girl came just as naturally as falling in love with her mom.

In that moment, I didn't just feel something emotional, I felt responsibility.

Calling.

"As for me and my house, we will serve the Lord.", Joshua 24:15

That's when things began to shift.

Not overnight. Not perfectly.

But intentionally.

Through God's grace, her strength, and my growing desire to be better, I started becoming the man I was meant to be.

Not the version shaped by my past.

The version shaped by purpose.

"Therefore, if anyone is in Christ, he is a new creation. The old has passed away; behold, the new has come." , 2 Corinthians 5:17

Walking with God hasn't been perfect.

It's not about never messing up. It's not about checking boxes or pretending to have it all together.

It's messy.

There are still days I fall short. Days I say things I shouldn't. Days I don't make time for what matters most.

But the difference now is I don't stay there.

"Though the righteous fall seven times, they rise again." , Proverbs 24:16

This journey isn't about perfection.

It's about direction.

Being a father, a husband, and a man of faith isn't about getting everything right.

It's about waking up every day and choosing to live in a way that honors your family and your God.

It's about refining who you are, every single day.

"Create in me a clean heart, O God, and renew a right spirit within me." , Psalm 51:10

That's what God's love does.

It doesn't demand perfection.

It invites transformation.

"My grace is sufficient for you, for my power is made perfect in weakness." , 2 Corinthians 12:9

CHAPTER 7: LEADING YOUR WIFE, NOT JUST LOVING HER

A woman is one of the greatest gifts God gave to man.

And like anything valuable in life, it takes intention to keep it that way.

I'm not writing this as a marriage expert. I'm in the middle of figuring this out just like you. Some days I get it right. Some days I don't. But I'm committed to learning, and if you are too, we're in this together.

I truly believe God put my wife, Kayle, in my life to shape me into the best version of myself.

And if I'm being honest, sometimes it feels like He's got a sense of humor with the situations we've had to work through.

When you first start dating your wife, everything is different.

You're intentional. You're patient.

You're thoughtful.

You're trying to win her heart.

You plan dates. You listen closely. You show up as the best version of yourself, because, at that stage, that's your mission.

And then life starts to build.

Marriage.

Kids.

A home.

A career.

All the things you once dreamed about become your reality.

And with that reality comes pressure.

Here's the part that catches a lot of men off guard:

Your wife didn't fall in love with a stressed out, overwhelmed version of you who feels entitled to a meal and a break at the end of the day.

She fell in love with the man who had time for her.

The man who pursued her.

The man who made her feel seen.

"Husbands, love your wives, just as Christ loved the church and gave himself up for her." , Ephesians 5:25

That kind of love isn't passive.

It's intentional. It's sacrificial. It leads.

If you ignore this long enough, you'll start hearing about it.

Less connection.

More tension.

More distance.

But the real danger isn't when she's telling you something is wrong.

It's when she stops saying anything at all.

Because silence doesn't mean peace.

It often means she's starting to disconnect.

As men, it's our responsibility to lead our marriages back to a healthy place.

Not control. Not dominate.

Lead.

That means paying attention.

That means taking ownership.

That means stepping up before things fall apart.

"Look carefully then how you walk… making the best use of the time.", Ephesians 5:15– 16

A lot of us end up in a season where marriage starts to feel like two roommates living under the same roof.

It's common.

New babies.

Busy seasons at work.

Life stacking responsibilities faster than you can manage them.

You stop connecting, and start coexisting.

So how do you fix it?

You go back.

Back to what worked in the beginning.

Not just doing chores without complaining, that's baseline. That's expected.

If you want to rebuild connection, you have to bring back the version of yourself she fell in love with.

Plan the date.

Leave the note.

Make the effort.

Be intentional again.

"Let all that you do be done in love." , 1 Corinthians 16:14

Yes, it takes effort.

And no, life doesn't slow down just because you decide to focus on your marriage.

Work still needs to get done.

Kids still need attention.

Stress doesn't disappear overnight.

But here's the reality:

Your marriage is either something you invest in, or something that slowly drifts apart.

There isn't really a middle ground.

And here's the hard truth:

It's not your fault that life gets busy.

But it *is* your responsibility to lead through it.

Not 50/50.

Sometimes it's 80/20.

Sometimes it's 90/10.

There will be seasons where you have to carry more, and seasons where she will too.

That's what commitment looks like.

"Two are better than one… If either of them falls down, one can help the other up.",

Ecclesiastes 4:9–10

God didn't put your wife in your life to make things easy.

He put her there to refine you.

To challenge you.

To grow you.

To expose the areas where you need to step up.

And that's not always comfortable.

Sometimes it doesn't feel fair.

But growth rarely does.

If things feel distant right now, don't overcomplicate it.

- Start small, but be consistent.
- Show up with a better attitude
- Make time, even when it's inconvenient
- Speak with intention
- Create moments instead of waiting for them
- Most importantly, don't give up.

"Let us not grow weary of doing good, for in due season we will reap, if we do not give up." , Galatians 6:9

Your wife isn't expecting perfection.

She's waiting for effort.

She fell in love with the best version of you once.

And whether she says it or not, she's hoping to see that version again.

You don't need to become someone new.

You just need to become intentional again.

And if you stay consistent…

You'll be surprised how quickly things can come back to life.

CHAPTER 8: DISCIPLINE AND PATIENCE UNDER PRESSURE

"Love is patient, love is kind." , 1 Corinthians 13:4

The era of the belt and the wooden spoon is behind us. At least, it should be.

That doesn't mean discipline goes away. It just means we need to do it better.

You know the scene.

You walk in after a long day, and it's chaos.

The living room looks like a tornado hit it. One kid's half-dressed, another is crying about something that doesn't make sense, and your wife has that look, the one that tells you everything you need to know without saying a word.

You just stepped into game time.

Objective one: give your wife a break.

Give her a kiss. Get a quick rundown of what the day looked like. Then step in and let her step out, even if it's just for a few minutes to breathe.

Dinner can wait.

Or better yet, take initiative and get it started.

I get it, you've had a long day too.

But there's a difference.

You spent your day working with (hopefully) reasonable adults, solving problems, and completing tasks.

She just spent the last ten hours:

- Negotiating with a toddler over a third banana
- Explaining to a ten-year-old why she doesn't need a phone yet
- Managing meltdown after meltdown over things like a "missing" toy that was exactly where it was left

That's a different kind of pressure.

As men, it's our job to lead our homes, even after we've already put in a full day.

And that leadership shows up most clearly in how we handle discipline.

When correction is needed, keeping your cool is everything.

Reacting out of frustration might get immediate results, but it doesn't build understanding.

Fear-based discipline teaches your child to avoid getting caught.

It doesn't teach them *why* the behavior is wrong.

"Fathers, do not provoke your children to anger, but bring them up in the discipline and instruction of the Lord.", Ephesians 6:4

In our house, discipline is a process.

For our younger kids, stronger consequences are a last resort, and becoming more rare as they grow.

The goal isn't control.

The goal is understanding.

We're not raising kids who behave when we're watching.

We're raising kids who make good choices when we're not there.

I used to justify a harsher approach by saying:

"I'm not here to be their friend, I'm here to prepare them for the real world." There's a piece of truth in that.

But it's incomplete.

Because preparing them for the real world doesn't mean leading with fear.

It means teaching them how to think, how to respond, and how to grow from mistakes.

There are times you need to be firm.

Clear boundaries matter.

Structure matters.

You can't let the inmates run the asylum.

But there are also moments that require patience, where slowing down and explaining *why* something isn't okay creates a much deeper impact than reacting quickly.

The more you lead with understanding, the less often you'll need to escalate.

This isn't easy.

And if you think my house runs perfectly, you've missed the point.

I'm still working on this.

Some days I show up calm and intentional.

Other days, I feel like a drill sergeant coming home from a high-stress environment.

And with three daughters, it's just as easy to swing the other way, getting wrapped around their fingers and going too soft.

That's the tension.

And that's the work.

The key is intentionality.

Even a half-second pause before you respond can change everything.

A breath.

A reset.

A choice.

"Everyone should be quick to listen, slow to speak and slow to become angry." , James 1:19

God didn't call us to be perfect fathers.

He called us to be present, intentional ones.

To lead with love.

To correct with purpose.

To guide, not control.

At the end of the day, we're not just managing behavior.

We're shaping people.

And the goal isn't obedience driven by fear.

It's growth driven by love.

THE FINALITY OF A NEVER-ENDING JOURNEY

I was recently talking with a client who, over the past several years, has been watching his father slowly decline. I asked him how his dad was doing, and he paused before answering, "He's okay… but it's been very tough."

It wasn't just what he said, it was how he said it. You could hear the weight behind those words. The kind of weight that comes from watching someone you've always seen as strong begin to fade. He went on to explain how difficult it's been helping his father with basic tasks, things that once came so easily. It was clear that, in his eyes, his dad had always been larger than life. A hero.

There wasn't a quick quote or easy response that could meet him in that moment. So instead, I shifted to something else happening in his life, something just as powerful, but on the opposite end of the spectrum.

He had just become a father. His son was eleven months old.

I told him, "I know it's painful watching your father go through this. But there's also something incredibly meaningful about being able to reflect on who he is, what he's meant to you, and now apply that to your own journey with your son. It shows you how important your role is. Forty-five years from now, your son may be standing in your shoes, thinking about you, your life, and what you meant to him. And the opportunity to shape that story starts right now."

He smiled. Not because it made things easier, but because it gave those difficult emotions somewhere to go. A sense of purpose. A way to carry forward what matters.

That's the strange and beautiful truth about fatherhood; it exists in both directions at once. We are always someone's son, even as we become someone's father.

And one day, whether we're ready for it or not, the roles shift.

The reality is this: there will come a day, suddenly, and without warning, when the story begins to close. And when it does, the question won't be whether memories exist. The question will be which ones remain.

Are they filled with warmth and laughter?

With guidance and presence? Or with distance, regret, and things left unsaid?

A man's true legacy isn't measured in dollars, titles, or accomplishments. It lives on in what he passes down, his character, his values, his wisdom, and the way he made people feel.

The client I was speaking with comes from a family of significant success. His father built wealth, businesses, and a life many would admire from the outside. And while those achievements still matter, they weren't what filled his mind as he watched his father in these final stages.

What he remembered were the moments.

A fishing trip when he was twelve. Conversations around a quiet campfire, just the two of them.

Early mornings with coffee, talking about business, life, and what it meant to step into fatherhood himself.

That's what lasts.

Not the resume. Not the numbers. Not the accolades.

The moments.

Fatherhood is a never-ending journey, but life itself is not. And that's what gives this role its weight, and its meaning. Every day you have is an opportunity to build something that will outlive you. To create moments that your children will carry with them long after you're gone.

The time isn't later. It's not when work slows down or when life gets easier.

The time is now.

Build the legacy.

Be present in the moments that matter. Show your children what love, strength, and guidance look like in real time.

Make it easy for them, one day, to remember you with fondness.

Because when that moment inevitably comes, those memories will be your greatest work.

ABOUT THE AUTHOR

Jon Simpson is a husband, father of three daughters, and business owner based in Michigan. His journey into fatherhood didn't come from a perfect blueprint, it was shaped by real-life experiences, challenges, and a deep desire to become better than what he had seen growing up.

Through building a business, navigating marriage, and raising a family, Jon has learned that being a great father isn't about perfection, it's about intention, growth, and showing up every day with purpose. His writing reflects that same mindset: honest, grounded, and focused on real-world application.

Father Figure is Jon's first book, born from a commitment to break generational cycles, strengthen families, and help other men step more fully into the role their families need.

When he's not working or writing, Jon is spending time with his wife and daughters, building the kind of life and legacy this book is all about.